BE CONFIDENT

A POCKET GUIDE TO ELIMINATING DOUBT
AND BUILDING CONVICTION

D1519552

BY ROCKY GARZA

This Is The Year For
Your New Book

Published by *Self Publish -N- 30 Days*

Printed in the United States of America
ISBN: 000-0-00000-000-0
Self-help 2. Confidence 3. Inspiration
Rocky Garza, *Be Confident: A Pocket Guide to Eliminating Doubt & Building Conviction.*

For my children, Ezra and Marlow.
I hope you both experience the goodness, truth, and beauty
in who you are and that you are constantly reminded
that truth wins over doubt every time.

TABLE OF CONTENTS

FOREWORD

by Carter Willis

When Rocky asked me to write the foreword to his book, I had a "Come again?" moment. I immediately wanted to let him know—for the sake of the good work he was about to publish—that asking a friend to endorse your book might not be the most lucrative idea.

Yes, I'm pursuing a doctorate in higher education that would give me a fancier title, but I do not yet have that illustrious prefix. Who would take my word that what they were about to read would be valuable to their well-being well beyond the final chapter?

They may believe that I'm only saying great things about Rocky because I am his friend. But, before I could drown in all the reasons I felt inadequate, I experienced something incredible: meta-doubt.

There I was. Directly in the middle of the experience that my friend, Rocky, was not only keenly aware of but was ready to destroy—for himself and for me. For you.

Though I may have thought I had an effective security system in place, doubt walked right through the door. I was fabricating reasons I shouldn't or couldn't contribute a published piece for Rocky's helpful text. My own doubt was confirmation of the need for what Rocky had to offer.

I've seen Rocky work. His work takes many forms, be it conference calls, coaching sessions, speaking engagements, the list goes on. My favorite moments are when Rocky closes his eyes or stares at the ceiling. He just starts dropping a firehose of knowledge as if he's reading the backs of his eyelids or reciting words from the ceiling tiles.

Be Confident is a book that is full of my favorite moments. Rocky has finally put pen to page and shares a tangible representation of the clarity that only he can provide. He understands that what he has to share is not an end-all, be-all, and he aims to be vulnerable with you.

Rocky's main desire is that you simply come along. He is the teacher who is willing to walk you through the homework.

I teach communication at Dallas Baptist University and direct the master's program for the same subject. No matter the classroom, be it full of eighteen-year-olds fresh from high school or a mix of generations (many of them older than me), I set a specific and pointed ground rule: no disclaimers.

My attempt at ensuring the cultivation of confidence came naturally. It was born from so many people's tendencies to hold back, including my own (see paragraph one of this foreword for reference).

Rocky's words are meant to bring clarity to why we create disclaimers. Rocky has observed and experienced countless moments of disconnect between who we really are and who someone else told us we were. He believes that, by differentiating the two, we will unlock entirely new levels of our stories. His book should help you find doubt and put a target on its back.

Believe me when I tell you that reading Rocky's book gave me the confidence to write this foreword. My very words are a testament to the legitimacy of what my dear friend has to say.

PROLOGUE

Let me start by saying two things.

First, thank you! From the bottom of my heart, thank you. I cannot tell you how much it means to me to have your support. There are a million books you could be reading right now, but you chose this one. Thank you.

Secondly, you are in the right place. Something you've read briefly has resonated with you. Somewhere, a chord was struck. You had a moment of courage and belief in yourself to begin the work required to kill doubt and build conviction. And for that, I am proud of you.

This little book is designed to be your daily companion. I by no means believe that the process of killing doubt is a one-time deal. That simply isn't possible.

We can't kill doubt, fear, insecurities, pain, hurt, or any false narratives in one fell swoop with the goal of never having to think about them again. But I do believe that consistent steps in the same direction lead us to a path of freedom and connection. Consistent hard work can continually put us on the path to where we want to go.

Before we get to the nitty-gritty, there are a few things I want to address and mention to keep your mind in the right space.

As you navigate through this book, you are potentially going to uncover some areas of your life that you have shoved down, buried away, or forgotten. I don't say that to scare you or be overly dramatic, but to encourage you to prepare. We're not trying to get over the doubts we feel and the lies we believe. We're trying to get through them. To see the cycle that has played come to an end.

Don't lose sight of this truth: all of us, and I truly mean all of us, have doubt. We all have fears and insecurities, and we're all looking for freedom. So, remember you are not alone. There are thousands of others just like you who are journeying alongside you to kill doubt and build the conviction to live a life of freedom.

For those of us reading this book that fall under the category of both children and parents, we will need to provide ourselves the space to process both sides. To process not only the story that was written about us but to begin to understand the stories we are writing for those we love.

> We're not trying to get over the doubts we feel and the lies we believe. We're trying to get through them.

As we continue this journey, I will do my best to provide little notes, quotes, and thoughts for us to consider, especially as parents and caretakers. You have made a fantastic decision to invest in yourself. Now, begin by giving yourself the space and grace you deserve to start to kill the doubt in your life.

There are two things you are going to need as you work through this book. You're going to need space and grace. There is a whole chapter dedicated to this topic, so I don't want to give out too many spoilers right now. But I think this practice of providing yourself with space and grace is so important that I want to plant the seed now.

You will need time to process, time to grieve, time to sit in the uncomfortable, and time to heal. There is time for it all; don't rush the process. Be slow, be patient, be thoughtful. You're also not supposed to have everything figured out by now, no matter how old you are or what your life experience has been.

I won't allow any "I should be past this by now" or "This shouldn't be affecting me this way" talk. There is no room for "should-ing" yourself here. There is only room for grace.

My hopes and intentions are that you keep this book and this work with you for years to come. I hope that it becomes something you can consistently reread to remind yourself what is true. At every turn, give yourself space.

CHAPTER 1

HELLO, DOUBT

Doubt is dumb. I don't like it. I don't think that doubt is kind, and I definitely don't think it cares about you. But then again, I think that's what makes it doubt. Doubt is a tiny thief that secretly steals the beauty, the wonder, and the uniqueness inside.

Not only is doubt dumb, but it is also patient. Doubt waits. It doesn't pressure you or give you any sense of urgency. It sits calmly. Like a cougar stalking its prey, doubt has no problem waiting. It likes to linger for the moment for fear that you might begin to believe that you are worthy and valuable.

Then, like clockwork, it recognizes when you're about to take a step, make a change, and finally move in the direction you believe was made for you. It strikes. It reminds you of those stories someone told you. It reminds you of that moment you failed. It reminds you about all those conversations you've had with yourself over the last few years, where in the end, doubt convinced you that you were just not as good as you thought you were.

Does that sound familiar? Does that feel familiar? That moment where you're about to finally believe in yourself and, like a vapor, the belief just vanishes. I get it. I've been there, and I understand. It happens to me, too.

In 2017, a CEO reached out and hired me to speak at their annual leadership event. The event was for 500 sales professionals. Initially, I was ecstatic. It was an amazing opportunity.

I packed in a flurry, then hopped on the plane. As I sat in the cramped seat and tried to fend off the blizzard coming from the air conditioner, there was nothing but positivity on my mind. In that seat, I reviewed my notes with a smile.

I arrived at the event. Still feeling great, I strutted backstage. Then, right there, just when I was about to walk on the stage, I had one of those moments.

They chose the wrong person, I thought. *I'm not a good fit. Sales professionals don't want to hear about vulnerability. They don't want to get into their feels and look at who they are. This is bad. This is a bad idea. I am not who I say I am.* Doubt snuck in.

My chest tightened. My throat felt coarse. Suddenly, all the gumption I had on the plane and in the hotel room vanished.

Doubt has also reared its ugly head in my role as a husband.

After a tough day at work, a challenging conversation with my kids, or a situation where I have wanted to share the not-so-proud moments with my wife, I can start off with the utmost confidence.

I've thought about what I'm going to say. I've processed my feelings, looked at both sides, and was ready to vulnerably share who I was, what I felt, and how I saw her. And then, I felt the knot in my throat. *Don't do it. She won't believe you. She will leave. She will get mad. She …* Again, doubt snuck in.

I have spent a large portion of my life believing the wrong story. Now, to be clear, it wasn't intentional. It's not as if I woke up one day and said, "You know what I'm going to do today? I'm going to live my life based on somebody else's story of who I am."

But doubt is devious. Doubt came in so stealthily that it took an intentional moment of reflection to realize I was living a life that wasn't mine. There were moments when doubt, which had been so natural for so long, didn't feel like me anymore.

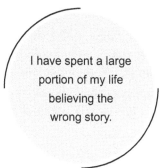

I have spent a large portion of my life believing the wrong story.

I am not the person who lives from a place of conviction, has assurance in my words, and then clams up with doubt right before a moment of opportunity to be vulnerable.

I am not the husband who, in the midst of working hard to build a marriage of trust and intimacy, panics when it comes to sharing his feelings. But that's who doubt made me.

Doubt found a way to sneak in and take control because I believed the wrong story. I had not completed the cycle of putting the doubt to death and crafting a new narrative. And, for most of us, we are living the wrong story, too.

We are stuck in survival mode. Survival is a beautiful thing. Survival mode is the very thing that has kept many of us alive up to this point and has been the one thing allowing us to walk out of tricky situations.

I am not knocking survival, but I do not believe that living in a constant state of survival is sustainable. It is not how we are designed to live. Instead, I think we were created for freedom, connection, and intimacy. We were put on this earth to live a life of deep conviction. Holding fast to our deep-seated beliefs without wavering from the truth and beauty of who we are.

I didn't always believe that I had the freedom to live a life of deep conviction or even know what my convictions were, and to be honest, it's still something I work toward every day. I have spent a large portion of my life surviving.

For me, it wasn't life or death. It wasn't about making sure I could find something to eat or have a roof over my head. All those things were more than adequate in my life. Not only did I have everything I needed, but usually everything I wanted, materialistically. Yet, even with all those privileges, I still felt like something was missing.

I have longed my entire life, no matter my situation, where I lived, how many times I moved, where I spent Christmas, how many Tommy Hilfiger polos or colorful Express shirts I had, for something always missing from my life.

Again, I had food. I had a home. I had many folks who loved me and cared for me. But, more than any of that, I wanted to know that I mattered. I wanted to know that my voice mattered. Hell, let's really say it. I wanted to be wanted.

When I look back at my childhood, I can recognize all the blessings I had, both materially and emotionally, but I can also pinpoint a gap. There was a longing to be understood, to feel secure in my identity, and for my voice to be heard and valued. I wanted the inside of me to match the outside that everyone could see.

I felt a lack of consistency. The absence of opportunity to put down roots and have a sense of home left me feeling lost. I didn't belong anywhere. It was as if I was floating through life.

Growing up, I felt like a shiny balloon sitting along a fence or a chair at a party. I was always in the room with the people I loved, but I felt like I was floating past everyone. No matter what I did, I was just out of anyone's reach. They could see me, I could see them, but we couldn't connect.

That led me to feel separate. Apart. There, but not really there. So, although I would get the connection-attempting comments like how nice I was or how fun it must be to have three different homes to go to, they could never actually reach me. I was missing something I so desperately longed for.

I ached to know that I was valuable for who I was, not just what I could do. I would dream about walking into a home that looked and felt like everyone else's. I wanted to have traditions. I wanted to eat the same food at every holiday meal with the same people sitting around the table. And not because those things are the only way or the right way, but more than anything, I wanted consistency and predictability.

To be even more transparent, my childhood left me with my defenses at the ready. As an adult, I didn't want to get caught off-guard again. Yet, I didn't want to feel like I had to stay on guard all the time, waiting for the other shoe to drop.

Soon, I understood I wanted a break. I wanted to believe that someone wanted to pursue me without me having to give an exorbitant amount of energy to them. It was in the middle of these thoughts, the little lies about who I was and what I needed to be loved, that doubt was born.

As I look back in moments of reflection, this is where I painted pictures in my mind that belonged to someone else, where I took the words told to me and about me and let them sit in the driver's seat of my life. Where I let doubt take root and create a narrative for my worth and value.

When a well-meaning eight-year-old stared at me and said, "You can't be on our team. You just moved here, and we have always played together."

All I heard was, "You don't *belong* here."

When I was in sixth grade, a mom lovingly asked if I would like one hamburger or two. Yet, what I processed was, "You are a large kid and kind of chubby, and no one likes the chubby kid."

Another time, a caring friend simply asked what exactly I did for work.

When I told them, they appeared shocked and exclaimed, "And people pay you how much for that?"

What I heard was, "You are fake and make up stories, then charge people too much money when they just need help."

The simple act of a caring father who chose his career over rest sounded a lot like he was choosing work over me. When he was only trying to show how much he cared through provision, all I could hear was that I wasn't important enough to be chosen first.

The simple praises of a well-intentioned boss consistently applauding me for all I could do and rarely for who I was sounded a lot like only my actions mattered, and who I was carried no value.

The simple direction of a church encouraging me to smile, clap, and always show my best side sounded a lot like there was no room for struggle, pain, or anything less than perfection.

Moments like these are where doubt forms in us. It's where it has formed in me. The narratives in your head might sound a little different than mine, maybe even completely opposite.

Regardless, it's possible to rewrite that narrative to one that is firmly planted in conviction. The stories we tell ourselves have led to the doubt we believe about ourselves.

Doubt lives in the longing. It lives in the wanting, the hoping, and the needing. In the wanting to be enough, in the hope of being known, and needing to belong.

Doubt has a way of feeling permanent. The more I discover, uncover, and dive into who I am, the more I begin to expose where doubt has made a home. And, once we've found the resident, we can start the eviction.

Before you move on...

Now that you have read the first chapter, it's time to reflect. Remember, the first step in building confidence is self-reflection. Taking what you now know, ask yourself:

1. Have you felt the desire to belong somewhere?

   Yes. I want friends who want me. And I sense that I also don't fit ideas anywhere

2. What aspects of the stories I shared connected with you?

   "they chose the wrong person" - imposter syndrome

3. What doubt-filled stories come to your mind right now? Quickly jot down your stories, spending no more than thirty seconds on each one.

   - I'm not actually incredible artist
   - I'm not "that good" at design
   - I'm ruining my kids

CHAPTER 2

SPACE & GRACE

Discovering who you are is hard work. However, uncovering and uprooting doubt is good work. I will always acknowledge how hard this work is, but I want you never to forget that it is absolutely worth it. Still, because I am aware of the strain this work may cause, I believe it's essential to bring in another one-two punch phrase I love: space and grace.

Space, defined, is a momentary pause to assess what is true. If we're going to make any traction in our ability to recognize who we are and where doubt lives, we must begin with what is right in front of us, where we are, and what is true. I find space so vital that I've woven moments of space for you throughout the following chapters. So, whenever you need it, take it.

This definition for space came to me at the beginning of the COVID-19 pandemic. I was trying to figure out what to do for my business, wondering how I planned to pivot as a coach, professional speaker, and workshop leader amid a time when we weren't even allowed to leave our own homes.

I kept running all these stories through my head, telling myself the pandemic was going to be short-lived, that it wasn't going to be that big of a deal and that I would be unaffected because the world still had to "do business."

I would find myself the very next day overwhelmed by the unknown and the fact that I felt totally out of control. This became a consistent cycle during the pandemic—days at the top of the mountain followed by days in the valley. I was scared. I felt alone.

> Days at the top of the mountain followed by days in the valley. I was scared. I felt alone.

I didn't feel like I could differentiate between the truth and the doubt. Doubt was telling me that I was not doing enough. Doubt was telling me that, once again, I was going to be a failure.

Everything was running together.

And then one morning, I woke up, and something hit me. I was in the kitchen enjoying my first cup of coffee for the day and making eggs for the kids. Sara was trying to squeeze in a quick Peloton ride before I went back into our office (read: bedroom) and locked myself in for the workday.

Coffee in one hand, spatula in the other, and notes out for the workshop I was about lead via Zoom and Facebook Live, I thought to myself, "I am going to die. Like I am literally going to die if I don't slow down." I had no idea what that meant or how I would slow down exactly, but I knew what I was currently doing was not it.

Spatula still in hand, I began to realize that I had been living life non-stop, full steam ahead, go-go-go. Sessions, workshops, and speaking gigs were falling off my calendar left and right. A two-week stay-at-home order turned into two months, and people were losing jobs.

I was in the mindset that as long as my calendar was packed and I felt busy, that must have meant I was productive, I was doing good, and I was okay. I had already attached a value to how my time was being spent, and, in a sense, I had totally forgotten who I was.

I was minutes away from going live on a Zoom call. Suddenly, my worries avalanched. How could I possibly make a rational, logical, thoughtful, meaningful, or appropriate decision if I haven't even stopped thinking *about what is true?*

But I knew I couldn't let my anxieties overtake me. So, I told myself that I was going to make some space. Well, figurative space, because my wife, five-year-old, and two-year-old were always in the house. But, nonetheless, I had to do something.

I decided to do whatever I could to create a little bit of room to look at what encompassed my life. Not positive, not negative, not good, and not bad. I just wanted to be able to do my best to look at what was *true.* And this played out for me both literally and figuratively. In this example, it looked like me simply addressing that there was no physical space in my life for me to pause. I felt like I was living a reactionary life.

Everything felt like it had to be decided, fixed, and dealt with right away. It felt like I couldn't breathe. So, I had to create some physical space. I had to get up a little bit earlier for myself. I'm not saying that is the answer for everyone, but because I assessed those true feelings I had, I knew I needed to create room to breathe.

For me, that required setting apart time to not feel the weight and responsibility of the world on my shoulders but rather create the space to look at the truth. I would wake up thirty minutes before the kids got up, make a cup of coffee, and get my calendar out. I would literally look hour by hour each day and ask myself if it was something I needed to do, something I wanted to do, or something I felt like I should do.

That allotted time would allow me to continue to make clear assessments every morning of my reality so that I could do my best to be proactive and not reactive based on information that wasn't even true.

If you're anything like me, creating space will feel awkward and selfish at first. Like a toddler trying to walk, I was trying to find balance. On top of that, slowing down to speed up felt like the biggest oxymoron I had ever heard. Ultimately, it felt like there were so many other things I needed to be doing.

I thought to myself, "If I'm going to gain an extra half-hour in my day, I'm going to spend that time working out, answering e-mails, or building out my business' five-year plan." Nonetheless, I stuck it out for a few weeks to build the muscle, so to speak.

About a week into my new routine, something happened. With the singular decision to get up thirty minutes earlier than I had before with no snooze button so that I could have a cup of coffee and my journal (groundbreaking, I know), I could see and feel a shift.

I didn't feel as panicked. I didn't feel as rushed. I felt like I could see things from a clearer perspective. I started to recognize that I was painting the worst-case scenario, then practiced back-tracking from that moment to see what I could do to prevent it from happening.

And what was happening was that it had kept me from seeing what was true because all I could see was bad. Looking back, what felt like a lifetime was more like ten days, and space began to give way to the recognition that I could prioritize myself. Therefore, the acknowledgment of my self-worth was not selfish.

We need to create space for ourselves. Many of us have developed a routine where we have not prioritized ourselves. There needs to be time to see what is before attaching a good or bad value.

We don't stop. Or I'll say, we don't like to stop.

We don't allow ourselves a chance to really look at the truth of who we are. Instead, we need to take a momentary pause to assess what is true before we begin to make decisions about our worth.

We base our value on our profession. We base our value on the money in our accounts, how many followers we have on social platforms, and external metrics that have nothing to do with our purpose or identity.

You'll notice how the next page is blank. That's because I want you to stop. I want you to take a deep breath. I want you to stay here, don't move on to thinking about what you need to fix. I want you to give yourself some space. I want you to allow yourself the opportunity and freedom to

You'll notice how the next page is blank.

journey through this, constantly reminding yourself of what is true. Not good, not bad, not positive, or negative. Simply what is true.

Now, the other half of the equation is grace. I have defined grace in two ways: externally and internally. External grace is the

ability to see ourselves in someone else, and internal grace is the ability to see ourselves in ourselves.

Once we give ourselves space, I believe grace should follow. Now I realize that the definition above may not be directly in line with the evangelical meaning of grace that some of us grew up with, but it's a definition that I want to use in this book.

As we begin to uncover the stories we tell ourselves, especially as we start to reveal who the narrator of those stories is, we will dig up some pain. We will most likely unpack memories from our lives that many of us have stored away and hidden.

Keeping things hidden away for so long is why those same things are eating us alive. We are going to have to dig deep and find the root cause of doubt in our lives, and that's most likely going to require us to not only have grace for ourselves but, when appropriate, to extend grace to those we love who have potentially harmed us.

Reflecting on life, I realize that not only were there so many moments that would've gone differently if I'd extended myself some grace, but there were times when living someone else's story hindered my ability to extend grace to those I loved.

As I think back, these are the situations that come to mind. These are a few examples of how, without space, I could have never extended grace.

My parents got divorced when I was two years old. For a long time, I believed it was because they didn't love me. When my dad chose to get remarried and live with my stepmom instead of my mom and me, it reinforced the belief that I wasn't loved.

My dad made those moves because he believed it was what was best for me. At this point in my adult life, I can confidently say that the reason my dad allowed me to live with my mom was that he actually loved me and not because he didn't want me. And yes, even today, saying that feels odd.

When I think about what I needed to begin to find freedom from what was painful in my life, to find freedom from doubt, I think about this definition of grace. So now, when I think about this story, I can see that I was only seeing myself in me and not in him too.

Grace says that now when I look at my children, I know I would do anything for them. I would sacrifice for them. I would lay my life down for them. I would do anything to make sure that they were given the best opportunity they could have.

And so, if I'm willing to see that in me and I'm also ready to see that in my father, I begin to understand why my dad did what he did. I start to realize that he also is a human. I even begin to fathom that maybe he and I are a lot more alike than we are different.

Maybe the story that I've been telling myself the majority of my life wasn't written by me. In fact, maybe when I allow myself enough space to assess what is true, I begin to see the truth.

My dad loves me. For me to begin to walk toward what heals me and not run away from what hurts will require me to also extend grace to my father along with myself.

Before you can jump into looking at the doubt in your own life, before you can pull it up by the root and eliminate it, you're going to need to learn to give yourself space and grace. You're going to need to allow yourself the opportunity to assess what is true, even when it is hard.

Start by asking if you are willing to extend grace by beginning to see yourself in someone else. Then, take some time to assess whether or not you can see your own worth and value in yourself. Do you know what your values are? Do you know what your strengths are? What does it look like for you to create or add a rhythm to your routine that allows you to have space and grace?

Think of a rhythm as a cadence. When you are riding on a bike, your cadence is how fast your feet are moving. Similarly, when you think about your day, the rhythms you create will be the speed you are operating. It probably goes without saying, but none of us are capable of performing all day long at a high cadence.

So, when you are thinking about your daily routine and the tasks you know need to get done, how can you begin to create a smooth cadence, consistent rhythms in that routine to allow for space and grace?

If you read this and your gut answer was, "I do not know how to do these things," well, you are in good company. We all need some practice at this. And that's okay, normal, and good.

You might need to make a habit of creating space for yourself because you may have never seen it done or created space for yourself before. You might need to allow yourself the freedom to make the necessary changes to build space. And yes, sometimes it can feel like we don't deserve freedom.

Freedom from the lies that we have believed about who we are so that we can, in fact, extend grace to ourselves. You might need the reminder that the pain and trauma in your life were not your own doing. That the hurt you may feel is not a result of your own failure or wrongdoing, but a result of somebody else's pain projected on your shoulders.

All of this is to say, be slow with your self-work and be kind to yourself. Give yourself whatever you need. How will you know what you need? Space and grace, my friends.

Before you move on...

After reviewing the chapter on space and grace, go through the below questions and consider what this means for you. Really reflect on how this can be applied to your own life. Taking what you now know, ask yourself:

1. What keeps you from creating space?

_____

_____

_____

_____

2. Identify one thing you can remove in your life to create space.

_____

_____

_____

_____

3. What is the most taxing part about extending grace to yourself? Additionally, what is the most difficult part about extending grace to others?

_____

_____

_____

_____

CHAPTER 3

STORIES PART I

Throughout the last few years, I have not only walked with thousands and helped them define a language for who they are, but I have also done the work of digging up doubt in my own life. I have exposed where doubt has taken up space in myself, where it grew legs, and why I believed it so often.

The more people I talk to, the more stories I hear. The more time I spend examining my own life, the more I know this truth: for many of us, doubt comes from two places. Doubt comes from the stories told to us and the stories we tell ourselves.

Lies define a significant part of our lives. So often, without realization, we believe misconstrued stories about who we are simply because we have never taken the time to identify where they originated. We have been trying to survive and cope and get by for so long that we have yet to take the time to dive into our own stories.

Lies define a significant part of our lives.

Some of the most substantial narratives at play in ourselves are those told to us about us. And this isn't just a personal opinion; this can be represented through labeling theory.

Labeling theory is the psychological phenomenon where the way others define us affects our behaviors. For example, suppose a child is called a thug their entire life. In that case, they are more likely to fall into a life of crime than a child of the same means and personality who was praised and encouraged in their youth.

According to *The American Psychological Association*, "although labeling can have positive effects by bringing individuals into treatment, it can also have negative effects of increasing stress and decreasing the individual's ability to cope with stress."[1]

In short, how people interact with us and the stories they tell us matter. These stories have been exposed to us our entire lives. Not only can these be stories that have come from someone else's mouth, but these stories can also be formed by the treatment and actions of others.

Motivational speaker Jim Rohn once said, "You are the sum of the five people you spend the most time with." You will begin to believe the stories people tell about you. Your character isn't solely decided by you. It's molded by your surroundings and experiences.

Many researchers have supported the theory that what we learn between the ages of six and twelve about who we are and what we need to do to survive significantly impacts our adult identities.[2]

So, when people editorialize our identities, their versions of ourselves begin to take root without us even knowing. They start to form into truths.

Now, I want to make one thing clear. Regardless of these nar-

---

[1]B. G., & Phelan, J. C. "The labeling theory of mental disorder (II): The consequences of labeling." *American Psychological Association, 1999.*

[2]Piaget, Jean. *The Psychology of the Child.* Basic Books; 2nd Edition, 1969.

ratives' impact, I do believe that many of them were well-intended, meaning that whoever told them to us possibly had excellent intentions.

They were perhaps trying to be kind, or they were trying to be encouraging, or maybe they were just trying to be silly to deflect from something painful in their own life. You don't have to justify the impact of someone's words.

If you're familiar with growing up in a large family, you know that means there's always something to celebrate. Birthdays, holidays, a regular Friday night. We would always find a reason to gather. And, in the family I grew up in, love was often shown through the kitchen.

Endless buffets of entrees, sides, and desserts that could easily feed an army. After a whole weekend of celebrating the big and small things in life, I noticed my mom asked me questions like, "Do you want one hamburger or two?" "Do you want seconds?" and "Did you get enough to eat?" at every party.

There was nothing malicious about her questions. In fact, I know now she had good intentions with her questions to make sure I was well fed. She was just trying to take care of her boy. The impact of those questions, however, has stayed with me my entire life.

I remember growing up thinking anytime somebody questioned me about my food intake (whether they were simply asking if I wanted seconds or something more malicious) that what they really were saying was, they think I eat a lot. They're suggesting I eat from the adult menu because I'm a "big kid." Here's the crazy part of this story: I *did* eat a lot.

More than the reality and truth of how much food I did or didn't eat, the story that I heard was, "I overeat. I am too fat, and I am so big." One second of doubt, of thinking the things people asked me were malicious, was enough to plant a seed of doubt that I'm uprooting to this day.

And this was a story told to me about me. Someone else's questions turned into truths about myself that have stayed with me for a long time. Not intentionally, but because I never came back to address the lie. I never attempted to identify, define, and decide whether or not the impact of those questions was who I actually was. I just believed the stories that were told to me about me.

I believed them because, well, that seemed easier. Our default response is to believe doubt. Succumbing to doubt is more manageable than addressing it. For many of us, doubt is all we know.

So, starting now, we will do our best to have no more default responses. No more "That's just the way it is. I guess that's just me," or "They were probably right." Those are reactionary responses.

Now, while they are reactions you should avoid, they are understandable. In the words of bestselling author Melody Beattie, "I am a reactionary." The instinct when things happen is to react to them. However, as Beattie puts it, "when we react, we forfeit our personal, God-given power to think, feel, and behave in our best interest."[3]

In short, we fall to our most basic emotions and lose control of feelings of inadequacy and doubt.

[3]Beattie, Melody. *Codependent No More*. Hazelden Publishing, 1992.

No more. I want you to stop believing everyone else's story for yourself. Let those lies die today.

During the intense first few months of the COVID-19 pandemic, I was doing everything I could to build connection and community. I started hosting monthly calls via Zoom for men to simply connect and talk about what was going on in their lives.

Darren Palmer happened to be on the call when I pitched this concept of killing doubt and building conviction. After the Zoom call, Darren reached out to me and told me how he worked in the publishing world, how he could help turn my thoughts into a book, and how much he believed in what I was doing. Then, a couple of weeks after that conversation, Darren shared something spectacular with me.

Darren's Story

I can't say enough about Rocky Garza and what he's meant to my life. His road mapping and training allowed me to view myself from a different lens to explore what I am actually doing with my life, the motivation behind my actions, and where my identity lies. He challenges me to question where I get my natural ideologies from to decipher whether my views are based on truth or from a situation, a circumstance.

Let me share a little bit deeper. I still remember it vividly. Saturday night, I was winding down a little bit past 8:30. As I was reading with my lamp on, my wife sat beside me with her laptop. The TV in our room ran for some background noise, and I heard my oldest and youngest sons in their rooms arguing back and forth. I had already told them that they needed to calm down.

But while reading a book and hearing them in the background, I put my book down and noticed an alert on my phone. And what do I know? It was Rocky doing a segment for a conference. During his speech, Rocky began discussing road mapping.

He then started asking the viewers provocative questions, inspiring me to examine who I am, why I think the way I do, and where my thoughts come from. I had heard him speak on this previously, but something about that night struck a chord with me.

Just then, I heard an outburst from my children's room. So, I rose from the bed and came to find my oldest son had just intentionally disobeyed me. The next thing I knew, I went in and had a bit of an outburst of my own. While my son's actions were wrong, I know I didn't handle the situation appropriately.

I was upset because I knew that he had intentionally done it, but I had control over my circumstance. Unfortunately, my frustration overread my best intentions, and after I left the room, my wife came to speak with me.

"Hey, you know what? I know they were wrong. I know he was wrong for that. But the way that you were sharing, the way you were talking, I think it could have been handled in a better way."

Part of me thought, *okay, here we go again with someone trying to tell me what to do.* I especially didn't want to hear the feedback from my wife. I know others out there can understand; sometimes, we don't want to listen to what our spouses have to say.

We have a different approach. So, I started watching myself. I was consciously aware of what Rocky had shared in that keynote, but I started watching my posture. I started watching the thoughts that I had.

So, I caught myself when I came up with the stereotypical excuses I had beforehand when I didn't want to hear what someone was saying. For instance, with my wife and me, the situation is unique. Sometimes, if something didn't align with my identity, I would blame it on our backgrounds. We both come from different ethnic backgrounds, so I would utilize that as a scapegoat for our problems.

I would say something like, "Well, okay, that's not the way that I was raised on these side of the tracks," (That's a Southern term for how marginalized people felt that they had to stay in certain areas of town because they weren't allowed in certain areas) or

"This must be how her type of people raise kids." Yet, taking a long hard look at myself, I knew this didn't have anything to do with my identity or culture.

Then I found myself looking at it from the perspective of, "Okay, hey, why don't you allow for me to parent the way that I parent. I don't get in the way when you need to parent the way you need." I felt like that was needed, but I was uneasy and restless, and I had to admit that to my wife, even though I didn't want to.

This was huge for me because I had to admit that I was wrong. And, for one, I didn't want to be. Second, I feared if I acknowledged my own fault, it might open the floodgates, and my wife would come to me with everything else she wanted me to change. It's not like I've got anything against my wife, but being married, it can be that way sometimes.

Still, I had to realize my family was more important than my ego, and not only was my wife telling the truth, but I also knew deep down (through Rocky's speech) why I did what I did.

So, I realized it wasn't because she was raised on the opposite side of the tracks, so to speak.

It didn't matter what her race was. It didn't matter where we were on the socioeconomic ladder. It didn't matter our level of education. Most importantly, what stood out to me was that I resorted to someone I didn't want to identify with when I spoke with my son. I shared something from an experience that I had with my stepfather growing up. I reacted and shared a term that came from him.

The alarming part wasn't that I got angry. It was that I had acted unlike myself. This led me to go on a quest to dive into what else I believed that wasn't really me.

What else was I passing on that wasn't even me? What sub-conscious behaviors do I present that I might not even like? What have I attached an identity to because of what others have shared with me? How do I separate other's influence over me from myself?

Whether it's my ethnic background, gender, or what I do for a living with being an entrepreneur and a business owner, how do my actions represent me? How do I want to view leadership with my team and my family? Is it the mindset of my predecessors who thought if they were writing the check, everyone simply had to do what they said? No. I didn't want that.

That's not effective. That's not who I desire to be because I believe in treating people like people, not like a number. I want to let everyone know that they actually matter. I want a culture of excellence and empathy, a culture of moving expeditiously, but also a culture of execution, enlightenment, and continued education.

One of our core values at Self Publish -N- 30 Days is win-wins. So, I had to realize that I needed to transition from the same mindset that I had as far as what I did in the business world to my family life, how I viewed my children, and how I viewed my wife.

I didn't allow those who came before me to dictate how I would treat my staff, clients, or others I worked with. But unfortunately, until Rocky opened my eyes, I had fallen for it in my personal life.

One night, a little bit later, I was with Rocky and a group of people. "Thank you for being who you are," I told him because more business owners and leaders need to hear this.

This is not something just for women. We don't need to try to shortchange or demise self-actualization. Taking a hard look at yourself is not only a feminine issue. Doing so doesn't limit your masculinity. It's the opposite. You're taking charge of your actions. I realized through this process that I did things that I wasn't even conscious of.

And because of Rocky, the identity mapping, his keynotes, and our friendship and partnership, it allowed me to transition. It encouraged me to go into the room and call my children together and apologize to everyone for how I had acted.

Then I shared with them the importance of questioning their reactive thoughts and actions. Finally, I spoke with them about how our first impulse isn't always the truest one.

So, if I could say anything to anyone reading this book, take the material to heart. This will change not only your relationship with your loved ones but it also will be a catalyst for change in your companies, your nonprofits, and how you leave a legacy in this world.

Thank you, Rocky. Continue to be a change agent, my brother.

///////////

What are the stories that have been told to you about you? Think back to a narrative told to you about yourself where another person might have used words like *so* or *too*. I have found that adverbs, like those two words, tend to lead us directly to the stories that describe us.

Anytime we remember someone told us that we were "so" *this*, or "too" *something*, we are staring back at someone's perspective of us. Whether these stories told to us are true, well-intended, or coming from a good place, they can negatively stick with us for a long time.

So, start to think about it briefly. When have you been told you are "so" something? Consider a time when someone has said you are "too" something.

What are the first stories that come to your mind? Think of these stories as the stories that were told to you about who you are. Write them down. When you read them, what did you think of first? We're going to dive into this much deeper in a couple of chapters. I just want you to start thinking.

As you go through these exercises, as your own stories pop into your head and you put in the work toward uncovering doubt, I want to challenge you to be slow. I want you to be patient and let yourself dive into your own story. We are going to have plenty of opportunities to dig up the doubts and truths in our lives. Just you, your shovel, and a small sift to keep the truth.

Let's get digging!

Before you move on...

With everyone telling us who we are, it can be challenging to dig into ourselves to find the truth inside the stories. Taking what you now know, ask yourself:

1. What are three to five stories that have been told to you about yourself?

_____

_____

_____

_____

2. Next to each story, write down the first thing that comes to mind when you think of those stories.

_____

_____

_____

_____

3. Looking at all the stories together, what stands out? Are they all from your childhood? Are they all from the same person? Are they the same theme?

_____

_____

_____

_____

CHAPTER 4

STORIES PART II

In addition to the stories people tell us about us, we also tell ourselves lies. Like when you hop in the shower to decompress, and within thirty seconds, you have convinced yourself that the entire world is against you.

Or when you're heading home after work, and your brain somehow brings you to a realization that everyone in your office hates you. These narratives usually get you to a place where you think to yourself, *I am doing a terrible job. I am not enough. I am not good.* Sound familiar?

For me, the stories I tell myself sound like this:

Rocky, if you go work out instead of going straight home, you're selfish.

Rocky, if you go out to eat for lunch, the family has less money to spend on themselves.

Rocky, you are too intense. Look at their faces; they don't like you.

Rocky, you are so emotional. Stop crying and just man up.

These are some examples of the stories we tell ourselves about ourselves. No one has directly told me a story that sounded like "you're selfish for working out."

That doubt is just a product of conversations with me. So let me promise you and encourage you with this reminder: a similar internal dialogue is happening to everyone, whether we want to admit it or not. We are constantly telling ourselves stories.

Humans talk a lot. Yes, even you introverts. Most of our talking is done in conversation with ourselves. No one speaks more to you than you do. We are all talking to ourselves all day long. In almost every moment of the day, we are saying something to ourselves. And what we say typically falls in line with doubt more than it does with a deep-seated belief about what is true.

What are you consistently telling yourself? What have you said to yourself that you have always taken for truth? Creating space for yourself right now to assess what is true about your thoughts, do you find that most of your conversations are doubt-filled?

Sometimes the thoughts that contribute to the doubt you believe will sound defensive. Sometimes it'll sound like a worst-case scenario stream of thought. Sometimes it'll sound like giving the benefit of the doubt to anyone but yourself. Sometimes, it'll even sound unsafe to believe otherwise.

Let me remind you that, when necessary, survival is a beautiful thing. Some of us have clung so tightly to what we thought was keeping us safe. We held on, kept our eyes closed, and held our breath for so long that we never paused to look up to see if we even needed to. Even though we are not designed to simply survive, we might not know how to get out of survival mode. Life is not meant to be lived choosing between fight or flight in every situation.

It gets exhausting when we are stuck in the mentality that every day is a fight to just stay alive, keep our heads above water, and try not to drown. And when we are exhausted, we quickly end up in a defeated mentality. We find ourselves giving up, drowning out the noise, and numbing what doesn't feel good.

Life is not meant to be lived choosing between fight or flight in every situation.

Even if we have a lot of physical energy, without emotional, mental, and spiritual endurance, we are expended. That is when it is challenging for us to see the truth.

When we are talking to ourselves, it becomes difficult to hear ourselves. Read that again. When we speak to ourselves, I do not believe that we can hear ourselves. The metaphorical angel and devil on our shoulders are not third-party, unbiased opinions.

You wrote their scripts. And, to me, that's where the stories get dangerous. Because, without accountability, we begin to give those narratives the power to take control.

Without unraveling those narratives, we can't give ourselves feedback.

Accountability is best served by someone else.

We can get in the car and can convince ourselves in and out of anything by the end of a twenty-minute drive. No matter what we choose, we think we are right. And, again, that's because the conversation is one-sided. We are just talking, and we are not listening. On top of that, we are exhausted because we have been wrestling with ourselves all day.

Put yourself back toward the beginning of the Covid-19 pandemic. Think about how you felt at the beginning and even throughout the pandemic. Many of us were at home and were trying to figure out how to navigate a new life in a brand-new way. Even for those of us who might have hit a stride or routine, we went to bed exhausted every night.

Why? Because we were trying to survive and convince ourselves that we were in control of something totally out of our control. We processed the news, followed social media posts (shoutout to the memes of 2020!), checked our kids' temperatures, homeschooled, ran our businesses, and maintained relationships.

Add to that trying to make sense of it all each day while talking to ourselves more than we ever had. For many of us, new truths were born during that season, and new lies also surfaced.

Do you see the relationship between survival, anxiety, fatigue, and the ability for lies to creep in and take over? So, imagine you are thirty-seven years old. You had a less-than-traditional childhood and are doing your best to create generational change for your spouse and children. You are at times making it up as you go because you have never raised children or seen marriage succeed before.

You have created your own businesses because you want to do something you love while attempting to serve others. You spend as much time with your family as you can. And still, in the quiet of your own mind, you feel like a failure. Like, no matter what is really happening, no matter what the truth is, maybe you are not as good as you think you are.

This should be noted: just because you are making it up as you go does not mean you are faking it. Instead, you are simply finding truths for the first time.

This metaphorical person we just described is me. Daily, I am attempting to remind myself that I'm not faking it, that I'm not a failure. That I am not a big scam, and I am not a walking lie.

But I recognize that that lie creeps up most often when I'm attempting to do everything independently. And even though I ultimately value vulnerability, that vulnerability is not about exposing my weakness. It's about creating a moment that allows me to be seen.

My hope is that, at this point, you can begin to see how quickly doubt grows. Take how my 2020 went as an example. I am already susceptible to thinking I'm not doing enough, regardless of my effort, because of the stories told to me by the actions of others. If I was not performing, winning, and showing I could be the best, then I was not enough.

I started with a regular year where my goals were to build up my marriage, have fun, make my kids feel secure, and run a successful business. Then, add in a once-in-a-lifetime pandemic where we were all scrambling, all the time, to keep our heads above water, which easily made us feel like we couldn't do it all and do it well.

Not to mention, a civil rights movement caused many of us white folks to remove the blinders and see the reality of the land we love and the broken system we have benefited from for so long. Add all of this together, and you've got a breeding ground for doubt.

We must create a break from that one-directional conversation we have with ourselves to really find the truth. We all have doubts, big or small. We have all told ourselves lies and have been told lies about ourselves, and we all need to be reminded of the truth.

- Who we are is good.
- Who you are is good.
- What you have to offer is unique.
- You are not alone.

What are the stories you tell yourself? Don't think too hard, but when asked about the stories you tell yourself, what comes to mind? What do you say to yourself most often?

Here are a few I tell myself:

- Rocky, you are too intense.
- Rocky, you are too emotional.
- Rocky, you are not qualified enough to write a book.
- Rocky, you are not manly enough.
- Rocky, you are too soft.
- Rocky, you will never be successful.

Need a little more help? Go back to the stories you wrote down that were told to you about you and see if there is a complementary story to go along with those.

Before you move on...

While imperative to push into the stories others tell you, you also need to deconstruct the falsehoods created in your own mind. Taking what you now know, ask yourself:

1. What are three to five stories that you consistently tell yourself?

_____

_____

_____

_____

2. What stories became your default for the truth?

_____

_____

_____

_____

3. Do the stories you tell yourself consist mainly of doubt or confidence?

_____

_____

_____

_____

CHAPTER 5

ADDRESSING THE WOUNDS

I know that my family deeply loves me. I know they care for me. I know they have provided everything they possibly could for me throughout my life. There is no question about their intentions. Their intentions were good.

I have aunts and uncles that are like moms and dads, who I lived with every summer from seventh grade until my junior year of college. They took me on vacations, let me live with them, and treated me like their own.

I have moms and dads who love me so much and would move mountains to do anything I asked of them, no matter the cost to themselves. They all tried their best to make sure I was always felt cared for, safe, and loved.

I have grandparents who have sacrificed for me in so many ways—taking me in and allowing me to live with them. Raising me as their own and never once complaining about any of the added responsibility.

And cousins who have supported me cheered for me and have always been a place I could go for an added boost of confidence or belief. I have always had people in my corner who wanted to see me win.

My guess is that many of you have a tight corner of support as well, even if it looks different than mine. Maybe your family looks more like a network or a community. Individuals from the places you've worked, where you went to school, your neighbors, anywhere. We have had many folks over the course of our lives who have loved us the best way they knew how.

When we uncover the stories told about us, I believe that the intent held by the person who shared the story was good for many of us. They were doing their best. Your family, whatever that looks like, can love you, try their best, and still add to the doubt you feel without meaning to.

Now, there is a big difference between intent and impact. The idea is that, even if one side or one party has excellent intentions, that does not mean the impact of their intentions was received the same way.

The hard part (for me, at least) is that I have to own the impact even when the impact is different from my intention. I must be accountable for the impact my actions or words have on others. As we move on, look for where you have told yourself that other people's intentions may, in fact, have been good, but the impact actually caused harm.

The stories told to us about us can be some of the most powerful narratives at play in the way we see ourselves. I believe the stories told to us become the foundation for much of our self-talk and how we interpret the way others see us.

We tend to take the stories told to us and weave them into our own DNA. The narratives become so entangled with our own stories that they end up creating a false sense of who we are. In this process, we end up losing the ability to see ourselves clearly.

To find a clear picture of who we are, we have to uproot the doubt. We must begin the unweaving of these false narratives about our lives so we can recreate the tapestry of who we really are.

Knowing yourself is fundamental. Know who you are, and don't let someone else's narrative define that. Don't forget about grace, and don't be too shocked when you begin to again see the beauty and wonder of who you are.

Now would be a good time to pull out your notes from chapter three, your list of the stories told to you by someone else. Digging into these stories told to you about you, what do you hear? Where have you allowed the insufficiency in somebody else to create insecurity in yourself?

When I look back on the actions of my loved ones while I was growing up, what was communicated to me was that I was not a priority in their lives. Again, I realize now that they had good intentions. I can create space and grace to see myself in them. And, simultaneously, the impact left me feeling less valuable. I believe potentially well-intended actions or words of others have created an impact in your life. What impact did they create?

Maybe for you, it wasn't so much about what was said but rather what was *shown* to you about you. As I think back, a few things come to mind that illustrate a disconnect between people's words and their actions.

I think about how people scrunch their faces up when I ask a probing question and how that communicates my potential intensity. I think about how easy it seemed friendships would fall away after one of us would move. It was proven to me that I didn't really matter to other people. When I don't ask for help often, I think about how people quit checking in on me, leading to me feeling alone.

Remember intention versus impact? The purpose could have been to not say much about who I was, yet those few words had a seemingly massive impact. If this feels like you, what I want you to do is think less about the actual words that came out of somebody's mouth and more about the actions shown to you.

What did you see? What were the consistent and habitual actions of those closest to you? What was the litmus test in your house for whether there was calm or chaos? For that matter, ask yourself what the litmus test is in your adult life for calm or chaos.

Are you a middle child? Do you know someone who is a middle child? Because most of the time, middle children have the same experience of feeling invisible. Even though there may not have been many stories about them directly with words, there were things communicated to them in the way they were treated.

Most middle children felt ignored at one time or another. Most felt like they were forgotten or looked over at some point and that it was their job to keep the peace because there was often chaos all around them.

Then, when they found out they could be the peacemaker, they ran with it. They found value in their ability to make peace. They found solace in the ability to blend in and get lost in the shuffle. They found that when they rustled the fewest feathers, everyone else seemed to be calmer. So, they blended in, figured it out independently, and got lost in the process.

This isn't every middle child's story, but everyone's story has been impacted by both words and actions. The stories told to you about you have been both direct and indirect. For me, I am no longer willing to stand idle and let someone else's story determine the truth of who I am.

I'm sure, at this point, stories are flooding your mind. Stories that have played repeatedly in your mind throughout your life because they were told about you. If you haven't yet, I want you to begin to write these stories down.

Take your time and be thorough. I want you to start a list just like you did in chapter three, but let it flow. Then, as stories come to you, write them down. All of them. Even if they sound similar to the ones you have already written, write them down.

Remember the space we talked about earlier? I want to provide a pause for you here and acknowledge that I am asking you to dig up things in your life you may have pushed down for a long time. Things you don't want to remember, things you don't want to admit, and even things you may feel stupid for even writing down, much less saying aloud. If you are in a place where you need to hit pause or take a break, feel free to do that.

Take a deep breath. Make some tea or pour some tequila, whatever your flavor. And, when you're ready, come back. But just promise yourself and me this: you will come back. You will not simply run away from what hurts you but choose to run toward what heals you, which often means running into what hurts. It wasn't until I was willing to do the work we are doing right now that I ever began to feel like I was making traction on the doubt in my life.

> There's no way we can dress our wound until we are willing to stop long enough to address the fact that we are bleeding.

I realize saying "addressing your healing" means "addressing your hurt," and that might sound a little contradictory. However, there's no way we can dress our wound until we are willing to stop long enough to address the fact that we are bleeding.

I am not saying that your life, your story, or your experience can be easily summed up into a single word like "wound." But, from my self-work and walking alongside others, going to the places that hurt provides clarity. That's where and when we're able to find what is true.

Before you move on...

Don't let the fear of heightened emotions cloud your ability to see the stories clearly. Whatever you may be feeling, create space to acknowledge where you are right now, then push through. Taking what you now know, ask yourself:

1. What do you hear when you read through your list of stories?

_____

_____

_____

_____

2. What do you feel when you look through your list of stories? Google "Feelings Wheel" if identifying feeling words is hard for you.

_____

_____

_____

_____

3. Describe the impact these stories have made in your life.

_____

_____

_____

_____

CHAPTER 6

DISCOVERING THE LIE

When I was told I was too emotional and too sensitive because I cried and was male, I believed it. When others told me I cried too much, I was telling myself I cried too much. Because I had never seen men cry, I believed those stories.

I had never experienced the freedom of emotional expression honestly and truly. As I look back and consider those two stories throughout my life, that is where I find a collision. The two stories affirmed the cultural story that men shouldn't cry, and then the lie told to me that I shouldn't cry. That is where the doubt was formed.

The collision of the two narratives reflected lies back and forth to one another. And, upon that collision, it created an impact. That impact was doubt.

The stories we tell ourselves, and those told to us, have fed one another, and, at many points in our lives, the stories have collided. When that collision happens, the seeds of doubt are planted. These seeds of doubt begin to take root because of the lies we believe about who we are.

At first glance, it can seem like two sets of stories have attributed to different narratives when they're actually more alike than they are different. I'll even take it a step further and say they are related.

The point where the stories of others tangled with my own is where I can pinpoint the lies I believed about myself. And for many of us, if not all of us, this is how it happens. We have so much information that we absorb, soak up, and sit in that we lose sight of truth.

We forget what we really want and find ourselves consistently looking to another person's approval, another person's version, another's person's vision of who we should be. I, like you, find myself in this position often and have to come back to this exercise to unravel the lies and find the truth.

When we don't address the stories, they begin to tangle themselves together so tightly that we can lose our abilities to recognize what is true and what is not. When it comes to your stories, where do you see how they correlate with each other? What are your unaddressed doubts? Where have those doubts formed into lies you tell yourself?

Candidly, I have always been embarrassed that I was overly emotional. I was embarrassed that I was the guy who cried. I was ashamed of being a sensitive person. I was mortified that it seemed like I couldn't talk about my family or my life without having an emotional breakdown.

I was convinced that there was something wrong. That, maybe because I was raised by my mom, grandma, aunts, and many female cousins, there was something in me that just wasn't right.

I used to tell myself to hold it in and not let myself tear up. I wouldn't talk about emotions. I wouldn't allow myself to be vulnerable. Instead, I would protect myself.

To me, showing emotions meant that someone would get me; someone would make fun of me. I didn't want to be the big kid that cried. That train of thought was so exhausting. It always felt like I was hiding something, and I was. I was constantly trying to be someone I wasn't.

By not crying, not expressing my emotions, I didn't allow myself to be myself. Even in the tiny moments where I was willing to create space, there was never room for any grace. There was never room for me to see myself in myself. There was never room for me to see myself in someone else; all I could see were the stories that had been told to me about me, and they were winning.

That message was killing me. It was exhausting. It *is* exhausting. And, for so many years, it felt like there was nothing I could do about it. It was just who I was. I was stuck in a pattern of recounting the stories told to me and then, inevitably, telling myself the same things. On repeat, over and over again.

As I think about those stories now, all these years later, I am met with a moment, again and again, to decide what is real. I come face to face with an opportunity to choose whether I will allow the voice of doubt to paint an incomplete picture of my worth or to sit in the tension long enough to see how the lies were formed and put doubt to death.

To complete the full picture of me addressing my own doubt and lies, I knew I had to make a move. I was struck with this thought in April of 2018: There is no way I am the only one who feels this way. I know I am not the only man in the world who feels profoundly and yet believes he shouldn't.

So, I took a risk. I formed Wiser Sons, a gathering of men who wanted the space to explore how they operate, who they are, how they feel, and live a life of cultivation, not conquering.

So, twenty-two men gathered for four days in May of 2019 and did the work of exploring our stories, uprooting doubt, and building truth. We spent eight hours on the first day going through a process called Identity Mapping™, where we created the clearest picture of who we were as individuals we had ever had. Then, we spent two hours every night around a fire for a time we called "Why & Rye."

During these sessions, we drank rye whiskey and answered the single question: why are we here? Then, we spent the next day in two-hour workshops exploring what we really wanted in life, what kept us from attaining it, and what lies we believed kept us from living a life we believed in.

On the last day, we spent our time looking at all the areas of our lives where we recognized we were attempting to conquer instead of cultivate. What I mean by that is that I believe for many of us, especially men, we have been lied to our entire lives and told that it's our job to conquer.

> We were not called to conquer; we were called to cultivate. We were called to stay in our garden, till the soil, and bear the fruit given to us.

To dominate our field and to make everyone around us submit. This is one of the most significant lies we believe. We were not called to conquer; we were called to cultivate. We were called to stay in our garden, till the soil, and bear the fruit given to us.

We spent our time doing a lot of similar work we're doing here, right now. The work of figuring out where the voices in our heads are coming from, which are lies and have contributed to the doubt we feel, and ultimately, which of them will win.

Finding your convictions will require you to take a step back and decide who is talking. Who is the voice in your head that is currently determining the truth as you see it?

As we uncover some of the stories told to us about us, we tell ourselves about ourselves. Who is the owner of these stories?

Are you hearing your voice (truth) or the voice that belongs to someone else (doubt)? From what I know and have experienced, the voice that is winning, that has taken root, that we hear so clearly in our minds trying to convince us of their truth, is usually not ours at all.

The lies formed from someone else's story of us didn't come from us. That feels obvious to say, but sometimes it's so hard to remember. Their story doesn't belong to us, and yet, at times, it still prevails. Somehow, the voice of doubt is the loudest.

That is because you are human. That is because you, like me, long to be loved, long to be seen, and long to be understood, and, at times, jeopardize the truth to believe doubt.

Our desire for connection leads us to believe the lies told to us. And yet, even when it pains us to face the realities of the detriment doubt can cause, you can choose hope. You can choose to lean in, find the truth, and stand firm. Choose to believe that the truth is greater than the doubt by holding fast to your story and releasing the story someone else wrote.

This skill takes daily practice. It takes the literal effort of asking yourself the question: Is this your story of theirs? It requires the consistent and daily work of identifying what the truth is.

In the midst of not knowing, feeling confused, and sometimes wondering what difference it might actually make, take space in your life to breathe. Then, take a step back, extend grace to yourself, and begin again.

Remind yourself that the truth will prevail, and your voice matters. Practice using it. Find places, even if it's just with yourself, to use your voice. Practice the public affirmation of yourself. Practice looking in the mirror and proclaiming that what you know is good. Remove the criticism and judgment of other people's voices and come back to your own.

Finding the truth of your doubt is not about removing everyone else; it's about having confidence in ourselves so that, upon the invitation of others, we are reminded we belong.

Before you move on...

Remember, any time our stories collide, an impact is created. You cannot control the collision, but you can control the impact. Taking what you now know, ask yourself:

1. Who is the voice in your head that is determining the truth of each story?

_____

_____

_____

_____

2. Identify the stories that match, where a story told to you and a story you tell yourself are similar. Tip: sometimes "opposite" stories are actually similar. When I was told by other people that I was too intense, I then said to myself that I had too many emotions. These narratives share a foundation.

_____

_____

_____

_____

3. What are the lies you tell yourself? Then, next to each story, write down the lie created from that story.

_____

_____

_____

_____

CHAPTER 7

FINDING TRUTH

T his is where the rubber meets the road. This is where you take everything you have learned, reflected upon, and worked through so far and begin to create your Truth Map. This is where you start to find your convictions.

There are moments in life when doing the work of identifying and digging up doubt will feel overwhelming. There are moments where you will want to walk away. But friend, I ask you to stay.

Stay in the tension, stay in the hard, and hold onto knowing that you are worth it. Remind yourself that the voice of doubt will not win, it will not prevail, and it will no longer define you. To be sure that doubt is not the driver, you have to stay honest, and you have to stay present.

As you work toward identifying and labeling your doubts, you will need to push yourself to look past the deafening voice that says, "No! Not you, not now, not good enough."

There is power in addressing doubt, in giving a name to it, and sitting with it. So, again, don't walk away. Instead, lean into what might feel silly or trivial because you'll find that time to be robust and influential.

Throughout my journey to discover doubt, find the truth, and live from a place of conviction, I began to see how my stories were all connected. When we look at the stories told to us, the stories we tell ourselves, and the doubt formed, it all follows a pattern. I'm a visual learner, and organizing my thoughts and stories helped me see where I had chosen doubt over conviction. And so, the Truth Map was born.

The Truth Map takes the stories told to us, the stories we tell ourselves, and creates space to find the collision. Where these two stories collide is where we find the lie that formed and fed into your doubt.

The Truth Map helps you find the moment when two narratives begin to entangle themselves into a lie. Once the lie is formed, we begin to doubt ourselves. Doubt about who we are and doubt about our value and worth. Any doubt not uncovered can wreak havoc on our lives.

Before we get into creating your Truth Map, I have mine as an example below. There are two stories, the one told to me and the one I tell myself. Together, they form a lie, and because of that, you'll see how I began to doubt myself.

I did my best to give you multiple examples that will not only shine some light on all our shared humanity but also provide some potential space for empathy. I want you to recognize that you are absolutely not alone and that I, like you, am on the ever-winding journey of self-discovery, too.

Rocky's Truth Map

Now it's time to create your Truth Map. Looking back through your notes from previous chapters, which story told to you stands out the most? You can write that answer in the first column. Below

	❶	❷	❸	❹
Story Told to Me:	Rocky, you are so intense. Calm down.	Rocky, you are a talker, not a writer.	Rocky, you are not worth choosing.	Rocky, you are the strong one.
Story I Tell Myself:	Rocky, you are too emotional.	Rocky, you can't even spell well. You can't write a book.	Rocky, you are a commodity to be expended.	Rocky, don't expose your weakness. You are the strong one.
The Lie:	I am not masculine enough to be respected or loved as a real man.	People like me don't write books. I am not smart enough.	Life is hard. People are flaky and don't let anyone in. They don't really love you.	When I am weak, I am worthless.
Doubt:	Men don't cry, so you are not a real man.	I should just stick to speaking. I will never write a book.	I better take care of myself and protect myself always.	I can't be weak. I must be strong.

that, write the story you tell yourself that collides with the story told to you.

When you have your answer to the first two questions, you're ready to identify the lie. Looking at your two stories, what lie was formed from the impact of the two stories? Only when you've traced back to the stories and the lie can you begin to uproot the doubt. Because of these stories, what is the doubt you have believed about yourself?

Your Truth Map

You are doing it, friend. You are doing the good, hard work. You are here, and that should be recognized and celebrated. For many of us, right now is a moment of massive realization. For what might be the first time, we recognize the thread woven through our doubt, fear, and lies.

This moment is one of my favorites in my work, the moment we look up and recognize the stories that were told to us about us

took root at some point in our lives and began to feed the story we were telling ourselves—the moment where it clicks.

The two stories collided, made a home, and began to grow doubt in our lives. We didn't even know it. We were just recounting the narrative, the story that we believed made us who we are. And now, hopefully, you can see that the doubt is simply not true. It is not true because you've also recognized the false truth you have been living in.

You are human. You are not broken. You are not bad. There is not something inherently wrong with you. Doubt keeps you from seeing your value, worth, and beauty. While you have let doubt make a home in the past, you never invited doubt in. That story was written by someone else.

I know that our natural inclination is to find a quick fix. But you and I both know that's not how it works because the stories told to us about us will never go away.

Just the other day, work had been pandemic-typical, which means I was at my desk on Zoom for a solid six hours, with a nine-minute drive home where I didn't really have any time to decompress from the day.

I pulled into the driveway, got out of the car, and headed inside. I knew that I wasn't quite ready for what I was walking into. There would most likely be the everyday home chaos that comes with kids being home from school. At the same time, I had to transition from the role of coach and boss into the intentional character of husband and father. Nonetheless, I headed inside.

As soon as I could literally and physically unload from the workday, my kids immediately wanted to go outside. So, what did I do next? Obviously, I went outside. I initially thought I could zone out a little from the repetitive motion of swing pushing.

Yet, my brain was still racing about the four things I didn't finish, the two people I didn't talk to, and the book I really needed to write because I had pre-sold copies of it almost a year ago.

Dinnertime came, so I whipped up something fast, gathered the family, and tried to really come in for some intentional time around the table. It was me, my wife, a five-year-old, and a two-and-a-half-year-old. I started with the same question I asked every night.

"What was your favorite part of the day?" I asked, hoping to move on to the second question we discussed every night, "What was one thing that you learned?" But no matter what I said or did, my younger child continued to roll around in her chair and put her feet all over me, trying to touch me with her pizza-covered hands and constantly interrupting me.

Out of frustration, when that little jagged toenail on her foot grazed my leg one last time, I raised my voice, pushed her feet back into her chair, and I told her to sit still. Her eyes locked on mine. She caught the frustration and immediately started to cry.

She wasn't crying because I pushed her leg back. She was crying because she just wanted to be close to me. She wanted to touch me. She wanted my attention. And then, not even thirty seconds later, as we asked our five-year-old what he had done that day that he was proud of, he purposely ignored everything we said.

And, as we attempted to describe what proud was, he turned around in his chair and covered his ears. So, of course, being that my mind was still someplace else, I snapped at him and turned him around.

"That's not how we act," I told him. "That's not how we treat each other. We do not ignore family."

I picked him up from his chair and walked him over the wall. I made him sit down against the wall because I wanted him away from me, and, honestly, I didn't want to even try to resolve the situation.

He immediately started crying. So, I sat back down in my chair, took one more bite of my pizza, and began to see what I had done. I walked over to him and grabbed his hand so that he stood up, and I took him into his room. We sat on the edge of his bed, and I pulled him close to me. He immediately jumped up in my lap and wrapped his arms and his legs around me.

He squeezed as tight as he could, grasping for anything on my body to hold on to, and began to calm down. I told him I loved him and that I was sorry for losing my temper. Then, I asked if he would forgive me. As always, he nodded his head and affirmed that he would, in fact, forgive his father.

When I think back on this exchange with my son, I'm reminded of what I hope this moment feels like for you. The moment where you realize that doubt has for so long tried to convince you that you're not who you think you are, simply based on someone else's story or one singular experience that you have allowed to define you.

Even though somewhere deep inside, I believe we know the truth of who we are, at times, we forget what we want and believe. We forget the truth about who we are. More than that, we forget that there are moments in all our lives that remind us of reality.

> Even though somewhere deep inside, I believe we know the truth of who we are, at times, we forget what we want and believe.

That night, I sat on the edge of that bed, and doubt tried to grab me. I was a bad father. I wasn't doing a good job. I was screwing him up. I wasn't patient enough. I wasn't intentional enough, and I just simply wasn't enough.

And yet, where I see so much beauty and hope is in that exact moment. There was the embrace of my five-year-old's arms, the wet tear dripping from his face onto my shirt, and the innocent forgiveness and acceptance of an apology to remind me of the truth.

I am good. I am a good father. I am a good and loving father. I love my children well. I do not have to live in the lie that I am insufficient, but I can live in the truth that I am enough.

You can live in the truth, too. I hope and pray you feel the weight and freedom of this moment right now. I hope deracinating the lies and dismissing the doubt that has taken root for so long will feel the same as the child in my lap. That it will be the closeness of love. That it will be the beauty of grace and forgiveness.

That it will be a reminder to wash away doubt and begin to build the truth.

You are good. You are a good father. You are a good mother. You are a good friend. You are a loving partner. You are a caring wife. You are good.

Before you move on...

The main enemy of doubt isn't confidence but truth. When we stand in the truth, it gives us the ability to find our confidence and recognize what is good. Taking what you now know, ask yourself:

1. What are the doubts you believe? Next to each story, next to the lie, write down the doubt.

_____

_____

_____

_____

2. Where do you see those doubts having the greatest impact on your life?

_____

_____

_____

_____

3. The last paragraph of this chapter is my list of truths for you. Create your own list of truths.

_____

_____

_____

_____

CHAPTER 8

BUILDING CONVICTION

Before we close the loop, let's remember where we started. Doubt is dumb. I don't like it. I don't think that doubt is kind, and I definitely don't think doubt cares about you. But then again, I think that's what makes it doubt. It's like a tiny thief always with us, secretly stealing the beauty, the wonder, and the uniqueness inside each of us.

Not only is doubt dumb, but I also think doubt is patient. Doubt waits. It doesn't pressure you or give you any sense of urgency. It sits calmly. Doubt hangs around for the moment that you might actually begin to believe that you are worthy and valuable.

Then, almost like clockwork, it recognizes that you're about to take a step, make a change, and finally move in the direction you believe was made for you, and then it strikes.

It reminds you of those stories someone told you. It reminds you of that moment you failed. It reminds you of all those conversations you've had with yourself over the last few years, where, in the end, doubt convinces you that you're just not as good as you think you are.

Does that sound familiar? Does that feel familiar? That moment where you're about to finally believe in yourself and, almost like a vapor, the belief just vanishes. I get it. I've been there, and I understand. It happens to me, too.

But not anymore. It is time for doubt to find a new home because doubt no longer lives here.

You've done the good, hard work of uprooting doubt, and now you need to build or discover the truth. The Truth Map we created isn't complete yet. I left out the last step in this map intentionally so that we could pull a greater focus on it. To make it a true Truth Map, we need to add an additional section: conviction.

I define conviction as a deep-seated, firmly established belief we are unwilling to waver from. I believe on the opposite side of every doubt is your conviction. In every story, we are presented with an opportunity to decide what we are going to believe. Are we going to accept the doubt, or will we live in the conviction?

For me, the opposite of doubt is not motivation or inspiration. Both of those are great things, but I do not believe they can consistently and sustainably overcome doubt.

Motivation is the movement of the mind. It is beautiful, but it only allows for a temporary change in what we are thinking.

Inspiration is the movement of the heart. It is also a beautiful thing that allows for a temporary change in what we are feeling.

Conviction, however, is more accurate as the opposite of doubt because conviction lives in our souls.

As stated before, conviction is the deep-seated belief we are unwilling to waver from. It goes beyond a statement of truth, but the added element of faith is what makes it personal. Part of what makes conviction a beautiful thing is that it lasts a lifetime.

Does conviction allow for a temporary change in our minds, our hearts, and our actions? Yes. But I have found that it primarily will enable me to stand on a foundation built on more than just facts. Conviction is what puts doubt to death. Confidence kills the lie and reveals the truth.

I recognize that truth is a weird thing. On the one hand, many of us have grown to believe that truth is the ultimate, the pinnacle. On the other hand, it is the single missing item in our lives that can set us free, and that, regardless of how it would make us feel if we just knew the truth, we would be okay.

On the other hand, truth sometimes is like beauty. It's in the eye of the beholder. We like to bend or change truth based on where we are and what we feel suits us best at the moment. Too often, we sacrifice what could be a small moment of hardship for a lifetime of lies, simply for a brief lie of false security and comfort.

Just because we have always believed something to be true doesn't necessarily mean that it is accurate. That doesn't necessarily mean it is fully representative of who we are. It doesn't actually mean that it is true. It does not mean it is our voice, our story, or for that matter, that it is us at all. So then, what is the truth in who we are?

Looking back at my Truth Map, the lie I believed is that I'm not masculine enough to be respected or loved. That men don't cry, and, therefore, I'm not a real man. The lie is that I'm not masculine enough to be respected and loved. But my conviction is that I am, in fact, a man. I am enough. I am intense. And I am good.

At the bottom of my Truth Map, my doubt is that I cannot be weak and must always be strong. The lie is that when I am weak, I am worthless and have no value to anyone. But my conviction is that I am valuable when I am strong and when I need help. I can ask for help. I am good.

Rocky's Truth Map

	①	②	③	④
Story Told to Me:	*Rocky, you are so intense. Calm down.*	*Rocky, you are a talker, not a writer.*	*Rocky, you are not worth choosing.*	*Rocky, you are the strong one.*
Story I Tell Myself:	*Rocky, you are too emotional.*	*Rocky, you can't even spell well. You can't write a book.*	*Rocky, you are a commodity to be expended.*	*Rocky, don't expose your weakness. You are the strong one.*
The Lie:	*I am not masculine enough to be respected or loved as a real man.*	*People like me don't write books. I am not smart enough.*	*Life is hard. People are flaky and don't let anyone in. They don't really love you.*	*When I am weak, I am worthless.*
Doubt:	*Men don't cry, so you are not a real man.*	*I should just stick to speaking. I will never write a book.*	*I better take care of myself and protect myself always.*	*I can't be weak. I must be strong.*
Conviction:	*I am a man. I am enough. I am intense. It is good.*	*I am an author. I am smart. I am enough. I am good.*	*Vulnerability is a strength. Others want to choose me. I am lovable. I am good.*	*I am valuable when I am strong and when I need help. I can ask for help. I am good.*

Giving language and words to doubt only gives that much more strength to our conviction. Words matter. The words we use to communicate to ourselves matter. The language we use to describe doubt matters. How much space in our minds and hearts we give to the lie matters. Even more than that, our ability to create a language that breathes life into our convictions matters.

The stories we tell ourselves need to be redefined by our convictions. Look back at your Truth Map and consider the stories you wrote down, the lie those stories reinforced, and the doubt you believe. What is the conviction which counters that doubt? What is the truth that establishes a deep-seated belief in who you are? Because who you are is good, beautiful, and authentic.

Below is your full Truth Map template. As you build your convictions, I want to encourage you to end every one of them with the same final statement. And I want that statement to be "I am good."

Your Truth Map

	❶	❷	❸	❹
Story Told to Me:				
Story I Tell Myself:				
The Lie:				
Doubt:				
Conviction:				

You are good. Regardless of where you may have been apathetic, despite your body's ability, irrespective of your past actions or of the circumstance, you are good.

Identifying the doubt in your life provides an extremely pivotal moment—a moment where you must decide whether or not you will see what is true.

A moment where you must decide which story you will live by and which story you will let pass by. A moment where you can decide whether or not you will let the threads of the stories weave themselves into doubts and lies or if you, through steady and consistent effort, will rewrite the narrative.

Brené Brown said, "When we deny our story, it defines us. When we own the story, we can write a brave new ending."[4] And

---

[4]Brown, Brené. *Dare to Lead: Brave Work. Though Conversations. Whole Hearts.* Random House; 1st Edition, 2018.

friends, that is what we are doing here. We are writing a brave new ending to the story. We are not going to allow doubt and lies to hold the pen of our story anymore. We will tell our story so that we can build deep convictions about our value, worth, and beauty.

We are writing a brave new ending to the story.

In all the good, hard work you do on your journey of self-discovery and healing, know that you are good. You deserve to be known.

As you begin and continue to walk in your truth, always remember that when that sneaky doubt begins to rear its head, you now have the tools to change the story. Change the way the narrative has been written about you and how you write it about yourself so that the truth guides you.

You are not the sum of the stories that have been told about you.

You are not insufficient.

You are enough.

You are good.

As I think back on creating this book, I had to use every chapter to remind myself that I could complete it. Now I know that may sound a little crazy to say at this point. Still, I want you to understand how important it is to give yourself the ability and opportunity to return to this framework again and again. I mean, I used the framework while writing the framework.

And so, I want you to feel encouraged that this is lifelong work. This work is the consistent unraveling of the threads that have built the tapestry we stand in while simultaneously weaving them back together in a more honest, authentic, and meaningful way.

I want to leave you with truths you can come back to, again and again. Something you can lean and rest on.

Know your value. Your value as an individual is not based on what you can do but on who you are. So, give time, effort, and energy to explore who you are so that when your hands and feet meet the ground, what you do is a replication of who you are.

Trust the process. I'm going to say it again. Trust the process. Take wherever you are in life and recognize that you got there by spending time getting there. So, give yourself some grace, and know that change takes time. It's not going to happen overnight, but it will happen much sooner than you think.

Phone a friend. Always feel the freedom to reach out to a friend. You were not made to do this alone. We were not designed to live alone. It was never in the design of this book or the design of our world for us to go out and do things alone. So, when it gets hard, when you need support, when you feel like you just can't do anymore, always phone a friend.

Look in the mirror. Yes, you read that correctly. Look in the mirror. When you are happy about something, look in the mirror. When you're frustrated with yourself, go look in the mirror. When you feel like you've let someone down, go look in the mirror. When you are feeling yourself, go look in the mirror.

I say this because I want you to be reminded that in every single one of those scenarios, even if our emotions are different, the person in the mirror is the same.

Self-worth is not selfish. If there's anything I hope you're able to leave with, outside of the ability to create freedom for yourself by unraveling others' stories about you, it is the ability to recognize that your self-worth and making decisions based on your self-worth is not selfish.

Before you move on...

It's time to take back the reigns and put doubt in its place. You got this. Now, step out into conviction. Taking what you now know, ask yourself:

1. What is the lie that planted a seed of doubt in you?

_____

_____

_____

_____

2. What is the doubt you're no longer willing to let live as truth in your life?

_____

_____

_____

_____

3. What is the conviction that counters the doubt to establish a deep-seated belief in who you are?

_____

_____

_____

_____

4. What are the practical steps you are going to take to live a life of deep conviction?

_____

_____

_____

_____

A doubt-filled life is one where energy is spent convincing other people, or ourselves, of who we are. A life lived with conviction is one where energy is spent living in the freedom and goodness of who we are.

ACKNOWLEDGMENTS

I have to start by thanking my wife, Sara, for her ever-increasing support and belief in me. She has the beautiful ability to listen to me, love me, and challenge me all simultaneously. I would not be who I am today or have the confidence I do if not for her loving me. Love you, babe.

Friendship is hard, and friendships as an adult seem to be even harder. And yet, my friends came in clutch for this book. I am so grateful for your encouragement. There's no way I could have done this without the consistent check-ins and accountability.

To Carter Willis, for being willing to take the first stab at this thing and be the first set of eyes on it after the initial manuscript was done. I cannot imagine where the book would be if you had not been willing to so graciously jump in and help me. You took the first leap, and I am so grateful.

To the team at Self Publish-N-30 Days, you are all amazing. Darren, I remember the call in April of 2020, and because of that call, we now have a book. I am here because of your push. Katherine and the editing team, you totally crushed it and helped make this dream come true.

To the many folks who were willing to answer my questions, give feedback, and help bring clarity and data to all my theories and opinions, you all are the best. Thank you.

Lastly, thank you, Chelsea. I know that with complete confidence, there is no book if there is no Chelsea. You have gone above and beyond with editing, adding, adjusting, reading, and rereading this book. You have spent countless hours on it and have been the true catalyst to getting it done.

There are not many people that I feel truly get me, trust me, and are willing to dive into the deep with me on crazy ideas—but you, my friend, have, and I am so grateful for you.

	1	2	3	4
Story Told to Me:				
Story I Tell Myself:				
The Lie:				
Doubt:				
Conviction:				

	①	②	③	④
Story Told to Me:	Rocky, you are so intense. Calm down.	Rocky, you are a talker, not a writer.	Rocky, you are not worth choosing.	Rocky, you are the strong one.
Story I Tell Myself:	Rocky, you are too emotional.	Rocky, you can't even spell well. You can't write a book.	Rocky, you are a commodity to be expended.	Rocky, don't expose your weakness. You are the strong one.
The Lie:	I am not masculine enough to be respected or loved as a real man.	People like me don't write books. I am not smart enough.	Life is hard. People are flaky and don't let anyone in. They don't really love you.	When I am weak, I am worthless.
Doubt:	Men don't cry, so you are not a real man.	I should just stick to speaking. I will never write a book.	I better take care of myself and protect myself always.	I can't be weak. I must be strong.
Conviction:	I am a man. I am enough. I am intense. It is good.	I am an author. I am smart. I am enough. I am good.	Vulnerability is a strength. Others want to choose me. I am lovable. I am good.	I am valuable when I am strong and when I need help. I can ask for help. I am good.